GW00771357

Family history in Southwark

A guide to tracing your Southwark Ancestors

by Leonard Reilly

Southwark Libraries 1996

© London Borough of Southwark 1996

Southwark Local Studies Library
211 Borough High Street
LONDON SE1 IJA

ISBN 0 905849 20 5
British Library Cataloguing in Publication data
A catalogue record for this book is available from the
British Library.

Contents

The London Borough of Southwark area shown on a map of 1846 by Davies

Introduction and booklist

Tracing your family tree has become an increasingly popular pastime. This short guide to tracing past Southwark families aims to tell you about relevant sources available, how the library may assist you in your searches and to give information on places for further research. It will deal in some detail about sources available at Southwark Local Studies Library and in outline about sources relating to the area but which are held elsewhere.

Tracing a family tree has given pleasure to many of those that have tried, but this is a pleasure that has been earned. Tracing a family back through time or across a single generation is unlikely to be achieved without a considerable amount of time and hard, careful work. It will almost certainly involve travel to appropriate record offices and libraries, expense in obtaining certificates or photocopies and time in letter writing and phone calls. It is like a jigsaw puzzle sometimes with pieces missing.

It is wise to start research with realistic expectations. Links with Norman knights or unearthed family fortunes are more than rare; indeed it is very unusual to trace families back to before the 16th century. It is best to start with known information or to talk to older relatives noting names, relationships, places and dates. It is also wise to read one of the general introductions listed on pages 3 and 4. Membership of a family history society will also be a useful source of assistance.

This guide gives only a short introduction to each source and does not tell you how to plan your research. The sources you will need to use were not designed for the use to which the modern genealogist puts them. Many were generated in pursuit of the work of local or national government. For guidance on their interpretation the staff at the library will be able to offer help.

The library is unable to undertake detailed research on behalf of enquirers. We are however able, for a fee, to look up and copy specified information from electoral registers, directories and census returns. We are also able to refer you to professional researchers who could undertake work on your behalf. There is no charge for using the facilities in the library, nor is any appointment necessary unless you are planning to visit on Saturday or wish to use a microfilm reader or CD ROM machine.

Acknowledgements
I should like to thank my colleagues at Southwark Local Studies Library, Steve Potter, Margaret de Bristowe and in particular Stephen Humphrey for their help. Stephen Humphrey has provided valuable assistance with regard to archival material in the collection especially concerning poor relief and has provided valuable suggestions on other parts of the text. Thanks also go to Shelia Gallagher of the East Surrey Family History Society who made helpful comments on the text. The book was designed by Carol Enright. The illustration on page 6 is reproduced by kind permission of the Marquess of Salisbury and the photograph on page 30 is reproduced by kind permission of Mirror Group newspapers.

Booklist

Those starting family history research are advised to look at one or more of the books listed below. Many are available at Southwark Local Studies Library, others at the reference library or from your local lending library.

Cole, Jean - *Tracing your family tree. The complete guide to tracing your family history.* Equation, 1988.

Colwell, Stella - *Family roots: Discovering the past in the Public Record Office.* Weidenfeld and Nicholson, 1991.

Colwell, Stella - *The family history book; How to trace your ancestors.* Phaidon 2nd ed., 1989.

Colwell, Stella - *Tracing your family tree.* Faber and Faber, 1984.

Cox, J - *Never been here before? a first time guide for family historians at the Pubilic Record Office.* PRO, 1993.

Cox, J & Padfield, J - *Tracing your ancestors in the Public Record Office.* HMSO 4th ed., 1990.

Crush, Margaret - *The family tree detective book.* Young library, 1988.

Currer-Briggs, Noel - *Worldwide family history.* Routledge and Kegan Paul, 1982.

Field, D M - *Step-by-step guide to tracing your ancestors.* Hamlyn, 1982.

Fitzhugh, Terrick V H - *The dictionary of genealogy.* Alpha books, 1985.

Gibson, J - *Wills and where to find them.* Phillimore, 1974.

Gibson, J & and Creaton, H - *Lists of Londoners.* Federation of Family History Societies, 1992.

Hamilton-Edwards, Gerald - *In search of ancestry.* Michael Joseph, 1966.

Hey, David - *Family and local history in England.* Longman, 1987.

Hey, David - *The Oxford Guide to family history.* OUP, 1993.

Humphery-Smith, Cecil - *A genealogist's bibliography.* Phillimore, 1985.

Iredale, David - *Your family tree and how to discover it.* Lutterworth, 1982.

McLaughlin, Eve - *First steps in family history.* Countryside, 1989.

Pelling, George - *Beginning your family history.* Countryside, 5th ed., 1990.

Steel, Donald - *Discovering your family history.* BBC, 1986.

Willis, Arthur - *Genealogy for beginners.* Phillimore, 5th ed., 1988.

Yurdan, Marilyn - *Tracing your ancestors.* David and Charles, 1988.

Rogers, Colin - *The family tree detective.* Manchester UP, 1989.

Rogers, Colin & Smith John - *Local and family history in England.* Manchester UP, 1991.

Webb, Cliff - *Guide to genealogical research in late Victorian and Edwardian London.* West Surrey Family History Society, 1994.

Webb, Cliff - *Guide to genealogical research in Victorian London.* West Surrey Family History Society, 1994.

Webb, Cliff - *National Index of Parish Registers vol. 4, Part 1, Surrey.* Society of Genealogists, 1990.

Humphrey, S. C. - *A Guide to the Archives in Southwark Local Studies Library.* Southwark Libraries, 1992.

There are also a large range of pamphlets published by the Federation of Family History Societies, the Society of Genealogists and others which give more information on specific sources or aspects of the subject.

Journals of interest include *Family Tree Magazine,* the journal of the East Surrey Family History Society and *Root and Branch* the journal of the West Surrey Family History Society.

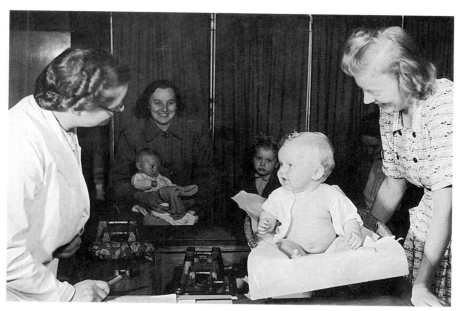

A child being weighed at the Bermondsey Health Centre in Grange Road c. 1930.

Joris Hoefnagel's painting of a wedding at Bermondsey. It probably depicts the marriage of the daughter of the Earl of Essex in 1566.

Parish registers

Anglican

Anglican Churches were required to keep parish registers in 1538 and of the ten ancient parishes for the Southwark area, six have registers that include entries for the 16th century. As the population grew the ecclesiastical functions of these parishes were gradually subdivided and there are surviving registers for an additional 72 parishes.

Southwark Local Studies Library is not a Diocesan Record Office and does not hold original parish registers; they are held at the Greater London Record Office. The library does however hold the following copies on microfilm. Dates have been simplified. The dates in brackets are the dates held at the Greater London Record Office.

Christ Church, Blackfriars Road
c 1671-1698; 1710-1751; 1770-1837; 1867-1933   (1671-1933)
m 1792-1803; 1807-1844; 1885-1941   (1792-1941)
b 1672-1837   (1672-1856)

St Saviour
c 1538-1571, 1653-1835; 1845-1852   (1538-1904)
m 1539-1571; 1653-1720; 1759-1835   (1539-1923)
b 1538-1570; 1653-1720; 1722-1835   (1538-1858)

St Thomas
c 1653-1687; 1691-1732; 1802-1863   (1614-1898)
m 1653-1687; 1691-1732; 1802-1863   (1614-1898)
b 1653-1687; 1691-1854   (1614-1854)

St Olave
c 1639-1665; 1685-1884   (1582-1915)
m 1639-1665; 1685-1865; 1908-1918   (1583-1918)
b 1639-1665; 1685-1853   (1583-1853)

St George the Martyr
c 1602-1715; 1758-1844   (1602-1923)
m 1602-1715; 1758-1837   (1602-1953)
b 1602-1715; 1758 1857   (1602-1868)

St Mary Newington
c 1561-1577; 1611-1810 1813-1836; 1843-1857   (1561-1960)
m 1561-1809, 1813-1836   (1561-1975)
b 1561-1577; 1691-1854   (1561-1854)

St Mary Magdalen, Bermondsey
c 1548-1603; 1675-1724; 1810-1856   (1548-1968)
m 1548-1603; 1675-1700; 1777-1785; 1810-1841   (1548-1967)
banns' books 1810-1822; 1857-1899
b 1548-1603; 1674-1688, 1810-1854   (1548-1865)

St John, Horselydown
c 1803-1863   (1733-1960)
m 1803-1863   (1733-1956)
b 1803-1854   (1733-1865)

St Mary, Rotherhithe
c 1556-1869   (1556-1943)
m 1556-1869   (1555-1943)
b 1754-1857   (1556-1878)

St Giles, Camberwell
c 1558-1750; 1763-1764; 1801-1845   (1558-1960)
m 1558-1750; 1763-1764; 1801-1837   (1558-1957)
b 1557-1750; 1763-1764; 1801-1845   (1557-1856)

There are surname indexes available for the following:

Christ Church	m 1781-1836
Saint Thomas	m 1614-1753; 1792-1837
Saint Mary, Newington	c 1849-1851
	m 1754-1772; 1776-1809
	b 1837-1854
St Mary Magdalen	m 1609-1832
St John Horselydown	m 1779-1837

The following churches' records are held elsewhere. Where no location is given the records are at the Greater London Record Office. The date is the earliest for which registers survive. In most cases this will be when they were started.

Churches within the ancient parish of Saint Saviour
All Hallows, Copperfield Street, 1876
Saint Peter, Sumner St, 1846

Churches within the ancient parish of Saint George the Martyr
St Alphege, 1873
St Jude, St George's Road, 1850
St Mary Magdalen, Massinger Street, 1843
St Michael & All Angels, Lant Street, 1881
St Paul, Westminster Bridge Road, 1858
St Stephen, Manciple Street, 1850

Churches within the ancient parish of Saint Mary Newington
All Saints, Surrey Square, 1866
All Souls, Grosvenor Park, 1869
Holy Trinity, Trinity Church Square, 1825
Lady Margaret Church, Chatham Street, 1884
Pembroke College Cambridge, Mission, 1886

St Agnes, Kennington Park, 1874
St Alban's Mission Church, Walworth, 1900
St Andrew New Kent Road, 1876
St Christopher, Barlow Street, *see* Pembroke College Mission
St Gabriel, Newington Butts *see* St Mary
St John, Larcom Street, 1860
St John's College Cambridge Mission, *see* Lady Margaret
Church, Chatham St
St Mark, East Street, 1867
St Mary the Virgin, Chapel of Ease, New Kent Road, 1894
St Matthew New Kent Road, 1864
St Paul, Lorrimore Square, 1856
St Peter, Liverpool Grove, 1825
St Stephen, Villa Street, 1866
Wellington College Mission, Etherdon Street, 1886

A wedding group of 1923.

Churches within the ancient parish of Saint Mary Magdalen, Bermondsey

Christ Church, Parker's Row, 1845
St Ann, Thorburn Square, 1866
St Augustine, Lynton Road, 1872
St Crispin, Southwark Park Road, 1874
St James, Jamaica Road, 1829
St Luke, Grange Road, 1885
St Paul, Kipling Street, 1846
St Saviour, Southwark Park Road, 1874

Churches within the ancient parish of Saint Mary, Rotherhithe

All Saints, Lower Road, Rotherhithe, 1840
Christ Church, Jamaica Road, 1840
Clare College Mission *see* Ephipany, Dilston Grove
Epiphany, Dilston Grove, Rotherhithe, 1886
Holy Trinity, Rotherhithe Street, 1838
St Barnabas, Plough Way, Rotherhithe, 1872
St Katherine, Eugenia Road, Rotherhithe, 1883
St Paul, Beatson Street (chapel of ease), 1850

Churches within the ancient parish of Saint Giles, Camberwell

All Saints, Davey St, 1892
All Saints, Blenheim Grove, 1872 (records in the care of the incumbent)
Camden Church, Peckham Road, 1845
Christ Church, Old Kent Road, 1838
Corpus Christi Cambridge Mission Church, Ilderton Road, 1891
Emmanuel, Camberwell Road, 1843
St Andrew, Glengall Road, Peckham 1866
St Antholin (Saint Anthony), Nunhead, 1865
St Barnabas, Calton Avenue, 1891
St Bartholomew's Mission Church, 1888
St Chrysostom, Peckham Hill Street, 1865
St Clement, East Dulwich (no records survive)
St George, Wells Way, 1826
St John's Mission Chapel, Lowden Road, 1893
St John the Divine, Kennington, 1868

St John the Evangelist, Goose Green, 1848
St Jude, Springhall Street, 1865
St Luke, Rosemary Road, 1874
St Mark, Coburg Road, 1880
St Mark, Harders Road, 1879
St Mary Magdalen, St Mary's Road, 1841
St Mary's Welsh Church, Camberwell New Road, 1912
St Matthew, Denmark Hill, 1930
St Michael's, Nunhead, 1865
St Michael's and All Saints, Sultan Street, 1878
St Paul, Consort Road, *See* St Mary Magdalen
St Paul, Herne Hill, 1845
St Peter, Dulwich Common, 1869 (records in the care of
the incumbent)
St Philip the Apostole, Avondale Square, 1866
St Saviour, Denmark Place, 1881
St Stephen, College Road, 1869
St Thomas, Albany Road, 1876
Wyndham Road Mission, 1876

Non-conformist registers

The Non-conformist records listed below are all at Southwark
Local Studies Library. It represents only a fraction of the area's
non-Anglican churches. Many Non-conformist registers are held
at the Public Record Office and a proportion of these have been
included on the International Genealogical Index (see page 14).

Baptist Churches

The library has received a deposit of marriage registers
from the Baptist Union:

Abbey Street, Bermondsey	m 1911-1942
Clifton Chapel, Peckham	m 1929-1971
Cottage Green, Camberwell	m 1924-1978
Maze Pond Chapel, Old Kent Road	m 1910-1935
Peckham Rye Tabernacle	m 1952-1960

Congregational

Emmanuel United Reformed
(now Christ Church United
Reformed and Methodist)   c 1889, 1891-1920
                                m 1893-1898

Methodist

Albion Street, Rotherhithe	c 1839-1883
Bermondsey Central Hall	c 1900-1964
Besson Street, Deptford	c 1850-1940
Deverell Street, New Kent Road	c 1840-1855
Dulwich Road	c 1928-9, 1941-66
East Street, Walworth	c 1911-1928
Gainsford Street, Horselydown	c 1842-1851
Locksfield, Walworth	c 1850-1955
New Cross Methodist Church	c 1874-1938
Peckham Methodist Church	c 1841-1954
	m 1867-1908
St George's Hall, Old Kent Road	c 1950-1962
Silver Street, Rotherhithe	c 1902-1915
Southwark Chapel, Long Lane	c 1837-1917
Surrey Chapel, Blackfriars Road	c 1876-1943
Trinity Street	c 1896-1899
Tustin Street	c 1874-1938
Zion Chapel, Neate Street, Camberwell	c 1856-1963

Roman Catholic Churches

Records of the currently 15 parishes are generally in the care
of the Parish Priest. In some instances the parishes and the
registers will date back to the early 19th century. Two chapels
date from the late 18th century, East Lane from 1773 and Saint
George's from 1786. The library has a transcript on fiche for
Saint George's Chapel: c 1788-1809
                                     m 1823-1837

International Genealogical Index

The International Genealogical Index, abbreviated to IGI, is produced by the Church of Latter-day Saints. It is a world-wide index to christenings and marriages. Not all parish or non-conformist registers have been indexed, this includes the majority of parishes in the Southwark area.

It is available at Southwark Local Studies Library in two forms. The CD ROM version called Family Search covers the whole of the British Isles. This allows flexible searching by surname, and searches can be limited by date or place. It is advisable to consult the Parish and Vital Listings (on fiche) or the *Phillimore Atlas and Index of Parish Registers* before searching the IGI to establish the parishes and period covered. Also available on disc is Ancestral File which records already established family trees. The IGI is also available in its older form, on microfiche. This is arranged by ancient county (Southwark will be in Surrey) and then alphabetically by surname. The library has the counties of Surrey, London & Middlesex, Kent, Sussex, Hampshire and Buckinghamshire for the 1988 edition.

Census returns

National censuses have been taken at ten year intervals since
1801 and those after 1841 include personal information. These
returns are released 100 years after they were collected.
Southwark Local Studies Library has microfilm or fiche copies of
the census returns for 1841, 1851, 1861, 1871, 1881 and 1891 for
the area of the present London Borough of Southwark. This,
with a slight exception of a small part of the Camberwell border
with the present Borough of Lambeth, is co-terminous with the
three registration districts of St Saviour, St Olave and St Giles.
The Public Record Office, which holds the originals, will provide
a copy of a specific address from the 1901 census to bona fide
descendants for a fee of £15.00.

The census lists all residents at a particular address, along
with their ages, their occupation, their relationship to the head
of the household, and their place of birth. The information
in the 1841 census is a little less full. Addresses are arranged
in the order the enumerator visited each area so it is common
to find streets, even short ones, split between a number of
enumeration districts. Street indexes have been prepared
to direct you to the appropriate film and folio number. It is
essential to have an address when searching the census.
Library staff are happy to give assistance on locating addresses
and on using the machines necessary to read the films.
It is essential to book a microfilm reader prior to any visit.

Surname indexes are available for the following censuses:

1841 Christ Church, an indexed transcript.

1851 All of the Southwark area. These are in the form of an indexed transcript for Christ Church, St George the Martyr, St Mary Newington, St Mary Magdalen, Bermondsey, and St Mary, Rotherhithe. For some parishes there are a number of alphabetical sequences to be searched. The indexes for the other parishes direct you to a folio number on the film. The parishes available in the form of an indexed transcript for 1851 and the index for Christ Church for 1841 have been prepared as part of a major indexing project called the SELON (South East London) index. All other 1851 parishes have been indexed by the West Surrey Family History Society.

1861 St Saviour, Christ Church and St Thomas. Prepared by the West Surrey Family History Society

1871 Peckham, St James, Bermondsey and Rotherhithe (parts only)

1881 All of the Southwark area. The 1881 Census Index was a combined venture between the Church of Latter-day Saints, the Public Record Office and the Federation of Family History Societies. The Southwark area is incorporated in an index for the whole of Surrey.

Pre 1841 Censuses

The censuses that survive in parish records are the working papers of the enumerator. They record various details for each family although not all residents or householders are listed.

1811 St Saviour, transcribed index at Southwark Local Studies Library to the original which is at the at GLRO.

1821 Christ Church (west division only) transcribed index to original at GLRO.

1831 St Saviour, St Mary Newington, Christ Church. Indexes and originals are held by the library. The St Saviour's volumes are unfit for production.

Civil registration of births, marriages and deaths

Civil registration of births, marriages and deaths started in 1837 and records, national and local, date from then. Certificates and their copies can provide the genealogist with much useful information. Obtaining such certificates is often the first stage in building a family tree. Records for all of England and Wales are at the General Register Office at St Catherine's House, and copy certificates are available from Southport. There is a duplicate set of records held at Southwark Registrar's Department. Full addresses are on page 38. For births and deaths they have been indexed for each quarter. For marriages there are locally held indexes for each church.

Indexes can be searched in two ways. Those at St Catherine's House can be searched in person free of charge. There is also access to the indexes at Southwark Registrars for the period 1837 - 1910. There is a search fee of £17.00 which includes eight verifications, each extra verification is £2.50. Appointments are advised. Staff are able to undertake limited search on behalf of postal enquirers for 5 years around a given date within one specified registration district.

A copy certificate is £5.50 from Southwark Registrar's, or £6.00 from St Catherine's House. From Southport they are £15.00 with no reference supplied or £12.00 with a reference.

It should be noted that the registrar's department holdings reflect current boundaries, so should a church move from one borough to another during a period of boundary change, so will the registration records for marriages.

Sometimes people cannot be traced on through civil registration. This may be because there was an incomplete transfer of records from the local to the national file, or because of non-registration.

Electoral registers and poll books

Electoral registers are arranged by address within wards and then constituencies. They can be useful in determining how long a family stayed at one address. Their value increases as the franchise widened.

Before 1918 the right to vote was a property qualification, but many people lived in property of insufficient value to qualify, or moved too frequently to be able to register. The actual qualification varied between 1832 and 1918. Before 1918 women had the right to vote in local elections only, if they fulfilled the property qualification. Women voters were therefore usually widows who had inherited their husbands' property, or spinsters who had inherited their fathers'.

Electoral registers are less helpful than may be supposed as, due to their poverty, the vast majority of Southwark's population was excluded before 1918. Searching the register is made complicated by the frequent changes in constituency boundaries and the frequent absence of street indexes. Sometimes it is necessary to simply work through the volume until you find the right address. Since 1832, boundary revisions have taken place in 1867/8, 1885, 1918, 1948, 1971 and 1983. New boundaries are only reflected in the registers from the date of the subsequent election.

Between 1885 and 1918 a single address can appear up to five times in the same volume, because of the differing electoral qualifications of the residents, so it is important to look under all the categories. Some properties do not appear at all, either because no one fulfilled the property requirements or the residents were too transitory to be registered.

The following registers are at Southwark Local Studies Library. The geographical scope, any divisions and dates of the constituencies are listed before the library's holdings.

County constituencies
1832-67 Surrey, Eastern Division.
Dates held: c.1832-33 Camberwell; 1847-8 Bermondsey; 1865 Rotherhithe.

1867-1885 Surrey, Eastern Division, included civil parish of Camberwell, none held.

Borough Constituencies
Southwark 1832-1885, covering the civil parishes of Rotherhithe, Christ Church, St George the Martyr, St John, Horselydown, St Saviour, St Olave, and St Thomas.
Dates held: 1839-1840; 1862-1863

Southwark 1885-1918, divided into three divisions; West, Bermondsey, and Rotherhithe.
Dates held: 1885-1886 (Rotherhithe only); 1887-1888; 1889-1890 (Rotherhithe only); 1892 (Rotherhithe only); 1893 (Bermondsey only); 1894-1895; 1896-1897 (Bermondsey only); 1898; 1899-1900 (Bermondsey only); 1900/01 (Rotherhithe only); 1901/2-1914/15

Counting the votes at the Southwark Election

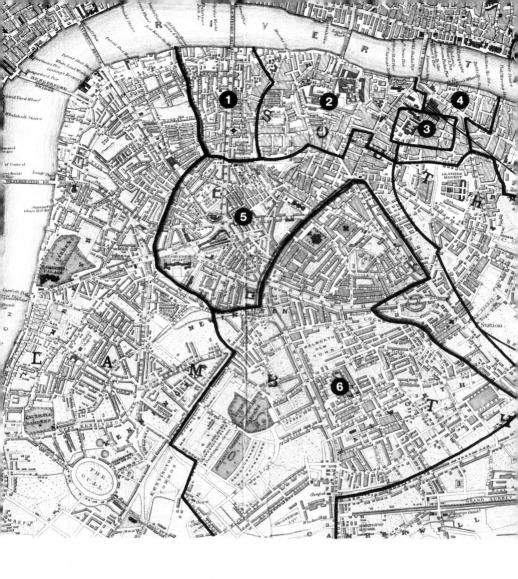

The northern part of Southwark from a map of 1841 published by Wyld.
The ancient parish boundaries have been indicated:

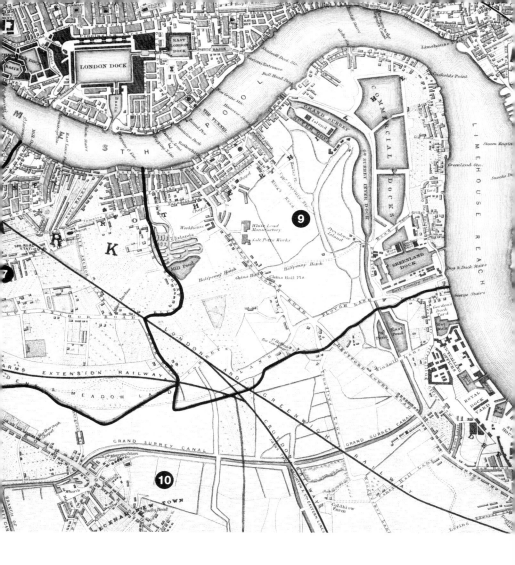

1.	Christ Church	5.	St George the Martyr
2.	St Saviour	6.	St Mary Newington
3.	St Thomas	7.	St Mary Magdalen, Bermondsey
4.	St Olave		

8.	St John, Horselydown
9.	St Mary, Rotherhithe
10.	St Giles, Camberwell

Lambeth 1832-1885, included part of the civil parishes of Newington and Camberwell.
Dates held: St Mary Newington 1833-1884 (arranged alphabetically by surname to 1879).

Camberwell 1885-1918, divided into three divisions, Dulwich, North, and Peckham.
Dates held: 1918-1923; 1926-1939; 1945-1952; 1955-1956; 1958-1964

Newington 1885-1918, divided into two divisions, Walworth and West.
Dates held: 1885-1914 (1905 Walworth only).

Metropolitan Boroughs
Southwark 1918-1964, divided into Central, North and South-east divisions.
Dates held: 1918 (and absent voters register)-1939/40; 1945-1964.

Bermondsey 1918-1964, divided into West (later West Bermondsey) and Rotherhithe divisions.
Dates held: 1918-1939 (Spring 1919 West only); 1945-1964 (1945-1949 include service registers).

Camberwell 1918-1964, divided into North-west, Dulwich, North and Peckham divisions until 1948 then Dulwich and Peckham divisions.
Dates held: 1918-1923; 1926-1939; 1945-1952; 1955-1956; 1958; 1960-1964.

London Borough of Southwark
1965 - divided until 1969 into Southwark, Bermondsey, Dulwich and Peckham districts and from 1970-1986 into Bermondsey, Peckham and Dulwich constituencies. In 1987 the Bermondsey constituency was renamed Southwark and Bermondsey.
Dates held: 1965 - date.

Electoral Registers held elsewhere.

Greater London Record Office
Borough Constituencies
Newington
1890-1913 (some unfit for production).

Camberwell
1890; 1891; 1892-1913 (some unfit for production).

Southwark
1890-1915;1918 (1898 Rotherhithe missing,
1908 West missing).

Surrey County Record Office
County Constituencies
1832-1867 Surrey, Eastern Division

1867-1885 Surrey, Eastern Division
There is also a list of voters resident outside Southwark or
whose eligible property is outside Southwark.

Lambeth Archives Department
County Constituency
Surrey, Eastern Division
1832-1887 Parliamentary voters for the parishes of Saint Mary,
Newington and Saint Giles, Camberwell.

Trade, street and telephone directories

Directories were designed to give basic current information on the area they covered. They were compiled in the earlier years by the publisher contacting clergy, Boards of Guardians and other officials. The quality of the information relied on the informant. There were no charges for 'ordinary' entries, only for specialised references or advertisements. They covered at most 16% of the persons living in London but the coverage is not even. There is a bias to the wealthier parts of Central London and the West End. Even the trades and commercial sections are incomplete.

Despite this they are a basic source used by researchers of all kinds, but particularly those interested in the development of a trade, or tracing the whereabouts of a person engaged in trade.

Many directories, especially the Post Office and Kelly's Directories, have a standard format which is followed year after year. These terms are used to describe the different sections in some directories;

Commercial - alphabetical listing of traders by their trading name or surname.

Trades - alphabetical listing of classified trades.

Street - streets in alphabetical order listing the traders in street number order.

Court - alphabetical list of private residents, principally the upper and middle classes.

Directories also often contain information on other subjects such as local government, schools and churches. The Kelly's directories are so called as Frederick Kelly took over the copyright from the Post Office in 1837.

The following directories are at Southwark Local Studies Library.

Listed by year
1745, 1790, 1803, 1805, 1811, 1814, 1815, 1816, 1817, 1823-4, 1827, 1832, 1836, 1838, 1841-1990. (1841 to 1881 inclusive are available only on microfilm.)

Listed by Title
Universal Pocket Book, 1745.

Universal British Directory, 1790.

Johnstone's London Directory, 1817, 1836.

Watkin's Commercial and General Directory, 1854.

Pigot's London and Provincial Commercial Directory, 1823-4, 1832.

Post Office London Directory
Note: these are found either as one entire volume or split into two volumes, Street and Commercial and Trade and Professional. The coverage is the same. They cover the area of Southwark, Bankside, Bermondsey, Walworth and Rotherhithe. 1803, 1805, 1811, 1814, 1815, 1816, 1827, 1838, 1841-1990.

Post Office London Suburbs Directory
1860, 1865, 1876, 1880, 1884, 1888, 1892, 1894, 1896, 1898, 1900, 1902, 1905-1933. They cover the area from Camberwell and Peckham southwards.

Kellys local directories or "buff books"
In addition to commercial information these give a fuller coverage of private residents listed by street and alphabetically.

Dulwich 1884, 1891, 1899-1901, 1903-6, 1911-16, 1918-20, 1922-26, 1928.

Camberwell including Peckham Dulwich and Nunhead 1888.

Peckham including Camberwell and Nunhead 1899, 1922.

Post Office Essex, Hertfordshire, Middlesex, Surrey and Sussex Directory, 1855, 1862, 1874, 1878.

Post Office Kent, Surrey and Sussex Directory, 1882, 1887, 1890.

Post Office Surrey Directory, 1899, 1903.

Telephone directories
Residential   London 1972- date.
Commercial   Yellow Pages
                          Central London 1972 - date.
                          South East London 1972 - date.

Cemetery records and memorial inscriptions

Cemetery records

There are three cemeteries in the borough. Nunhead Cemetery was founded in 1840 by the London Cemetery Company. Since 1975 it has been owned by the London Borough of Southwark and run with assistance from the Friends of Nunhead Cemetery. Camberwell Old Cemetery was opened by the Camberwell Vestry in 1856, and the New Cemetery was opened in 1927.

With the closure of parish churchyards generally in the mid 19th century many of the residents of Southwark and Bermondsey were buried outside the area. Likely locations include Abney Park, Norwood and Brookwood cemeteries.

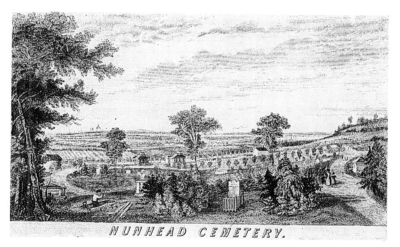

Nunhead Cemetery in 1840

The records of Nunhead and Camberwell (Old and New) Cemeteries are in the care of the Cemeteries Superintendent, Camberwell New Cemetery, Brenchley Gardens, London SE23.

Written enquiries will be answered when the name of the deceased and date of death are given. Personal searches are permitted.

The records are as follows:

Nunhead Grave purchases 1840 - date (indexed).
Camberwell Old Cemetery Day Book 1856 - date (indexed except for 1881 - 1910).
Camberwell New Cemetery 1927- date (indexed).
Crematorium 1939 - date (separate volumes indexed).

Southwark Local Studies Library has copies of the following records:

Nunhead Cemetery
Day order book, 1895-1896; 1898-1899; 1911-1912; 1933.
Register of vaults and graves, 1905-1910.

Tombstones removed from the churchyard of St Mary Magdalen, Bermondsey in 1930.

Churchyard and memorial inscriptions

Christ Church, Blackfriars Road.
List showing the positions of tombstones and monuments with inscriptions in the churchyard of Christ Church, 1898.

St Olave & St John, Tooley Street.
The remaining transcriptions of tombs in the public open space,Tooley St, formerly the burial ground, 1985.

St George the Martyr.
List of names on coffins and coffin plates found in the crypt and removed to Brookwood cemetery, 1899.

St Mary, Newington.
Memorial inscriptions transcribed by R Hovenden.

St Mary Magdalen, Bermondsey.
List of inscriptions on the vaults and gravestones in the churchyard together with inscriptions on the monuments in the church 1858-1860. Inscriptions inside the church as at 1841 in G W Phillips' *History and antiquities of the parish of Bermondsey.*

St John, Horselydown.
List of names on tombstones in St John's burial ground, 1881.

St Mary, Rotherhithe.
Inscriptions on stones proposed to be removed, 1903.
The inscriptions are also recorded in E.J. Beck's *History of Rotherhithe* chapter X, pp 134 - 158.

St Giles, Camberwell.
The disused burial ground, statement of tombstones and monuments, 1938.

York Street Chapel.
Monumental inscriptions, 1881.

Nunhead Cemetery.
Some grave inscriptions, North West Kent Family History Society, 1978.

St James, Bermondsey.
1819-1906 by C R Webb, 1976 at the GLRO.

Mr T & Mrs S Tansley of 186 Redriff Estate, Rotherhithe in 1954

Newspapers

Southwark Local Studies Library holds microfilm copies of all local newspapers from 1855. These may give notices of births, marriages and deaths and sometimes obituaries. Similarly reports of inquests are sometimes reported should the death have had an unusual cause.

South London Chronicle   1860-1907

South London Journal   1856-1871

South London Mail   1888-1906

South London News   1855-1861, 1879-1891

South London Observer   1870-1969
also called the Camberwell and Peckham Times

South London Press   1865 - date. Indexed 1865-1867, 1965-1988

Southwark & Bermondsey Recorder   1868-1933

Times 1785 - date (indexed), at Newington Reference Library.

Poor law records

The fullest surviving Poor Law records relate to the parishes of St Mary, Newington, and St George the Martyr from between c.1780-1830. The collection is incomplete even for these parishes, and little of the material has been indexed. For a fuller account of other Poor Law records (and other parish, vestry and deposited records) refer to A *Guide to the Archives in Southwark Local Studies Library* by S. C. Humphrey. Much of the material is housed in an outstore, and a week's notice is required before it can be seen. The Poor Law Amendment Act of 1834 had less local administrative effect than one would expect. The small parishes of St Olave, St John and St. Thomas were put together under a Board of Guardians as St Olave's Union and the parishes of St Saviour and Christ Church became the St Saviour's Union. The remaining five parishes kept their independence for Poor Law purposes until 1869. Only then were they merged into Unions. St. Mary Newington and St. George the Martyr became part of St Saviour's Union, and Bermondsey and Rotherhithe were added to St Olave's Union. St Giles Camberwell, on account of its rapidly expanding population, continued to be separate (eventually as the Camberwell Board of Guardians) until the end of the Poor Law in 1930.

After 1869 all surviving records are in the Greater London Record Office, as are many of the records created from the mid 1830s and some oddments from even earlier years. There is a copy of a list of these records at Southwark Local Studies Library.

These are the Poor Law records in the library which would be of most use to family historians:

St Saviour
Settlement Examinations 1794-1797 (indexed)

St Olave
Churchwardens' accounts, 1546-1591
Workhouse minutes, 1757-1783, 1795-1801

Annual register of parish poor children, 1785-1813
List of paupers, 1848-1858

St George the Martyr
Overseers' Accounts, 1635-1729
Apprenticeship indentures, 1677, 1752-7, 1760-1, 1764, 1768, 1776, 1787, 1799-1836
Workhouse minutes, 1729-1735, 1744-1771, 1795-1826, 1831-2
Bastardy Bonds, 1730-1830 (indexed)
Removal orders from the parish, 1743-1837 (mainly after 1810)
Bastardy Warrants, 1776-1832
Settlements disputes' papers, 1778-1831
Parish poor children in the workhouse, 1780-1807 (indexed)
Settlement examinations, 1783-90, 1798-1812 (original indexes for most volumes)
Register of illegitimate children 1797-1807
Workhouse admissions and discharges 1801-1832, 1837-8
Admission of the Poor to St Thomas' Hospital, 1803-1821 and to *Guy's Hospital*, 1776-1811 (indexed)

St Mary, Newington
Bastardy bonds, 1628-1756 (indexed)
Churchwardens' accounts 1632-1743, 1796-9, 1801-2, 1805, 1842-7
Removal orders, 1660-1742; 1847-1869
Apprenticeship indentures, 1675-1866 (listed in date order)
Workhouse register 1772-1784 (indexed; original unfit for production)
Settlement examinations, 1783-1846 (indexed)
Workhouse minutes, 1806-1852
Bastardy maintenance orders, 1808-1843

St Mary Magdalen, Bermondsey
Churchwardens' accounts, 1599-1625, 1676-1691, 1699-1794
Governors' and Directors minutes, 1748-1769, 1796-1811, 1818-1899

St Mary, Rotherhithe
Churchwardens' accounts, 1797-1890
Governors' and Guardians' minutes, 1822-1838, 1840-1850, 1854-1870
Letters received from the Poor Law Board, 1860-1866

St Giles, Camberwell
Board of Guardians' minutes (printed), 1893-1901, 1905-6, 1911-12, 1925-8, 1929-30
Reports on applications for poor relief or admissions to the workhouse, 1815

Taxation records

Rate Books

Rate books record payments to the local authority, the amount of which was based on the value of the ratepayer's property. Ratebooks can therefore identify the length of occupation and type of tenure of a person at a particular property. They can be difficult to use as they are unindexed, either by name or street and because individual house numbers do not appear until the mid nineteenth century. Ratepayers' addresses were generally listed in the same order in successive years so searching a sequence of years is not as time consuming as it might first appear. The following rate books are available at Southwark Local Studies Library:

Parish and Vestry

Christ Church	1820; 1828; 1843; 1849; 1853-1900
St Saviour	1748-1900
St Olave	1707-1900
St Thomas	1791 and 1792 only
St George the Martyr	1635-1900
St Mary, Newington	1673-1900
St Mary Magdalen, Bermondsey	1599-1625; 1676-91; 1699-1899
St Mary, Rotherhithe	1754-1900
St John, Horselydown	1734-1900
St Giles, Camberwell	1768; 1774; 1780-5; 1802-59

All rate books for the period 1880-1900 are on microfilm only.

Metropolitan Boroughs

Southwark	1901-1963 selected years
Bermondsey	1901-1963 selected years
Camberwell	1914-1964 selected years

Tithe Records

Tithe maps were compiled in the 1830's and 1840's to enable tithes, church taxes, to be converted to a money payment. Because the Southwark area was so urbanised at this time the only map compiled was for Camberwell. This was done in 1837. Accompanying the map is a schedule that lists landowners and tenants with agricultural land. There is an a surname index to the schedule.

Other sources

Maps

Southwark Local Studies Library has a large collection of maps of the area. The larger scale plans, if necessary used in conjunction with the London County Council's *List of Streets*, or directories, can be used to pinpoint addresses shown on certificates, census returns or rate books. The collection is a mixture of originals and facsimiles.

The earliest maps in the collection date from the 16th century and there are also estate, parish and tithe maps. Particularly useful are the Rocque map (1739-47) and the two Horwood surveys (1799 and 1819). The Ordnance Survey maps are summarised below.

6" to 1 mile (later 1:10 000) 1870 - date
25" to 1 mile 1870
25" to 1 mile 1894-6
25" to 1 mile 1914-6
60" to 1 mile partial coverage 1870 - 1947
1:1250 post war - date

For information on Tithe maps *see* Taxation sources on page 34.

School Records

The library has a small collection of school records. Only the following have any information on pupils, and this is liable to be very partial.

Zoar Street Charity School.
Lists of some scholars, 1687-1744.

Amicable Society's School, Rotherhithe
Minutes, 1777-1870.

John Street Sunday School.
Lesson and attendance book, 1838-1860.

Mint Street Sunday School.
Attendance book, 1883-1905.

The records of the London School Board, which was formed in 1870, and was responsible for the education for the majority of Southwark school children are generally at the Greater London Record Office. Some records are may still be in the care of the school secretary. The GLRO also has some pre-1870 school records.

Deeds

The library holds a collection of 25,000 property deeds. Despite this apparent size it represents a mere fraction of Southwark's property transactions. Virtually all those deposited before 1977 have been calendared and there are indexes to places and individuals.

Wills

The library does not hold an extensive collection of wills. Any wills proved before 1858 were registered at an ecclesiastical court. Local wills could have been proved at any one of the following:

Prerogative Court of Canterbury	PRO
Partial Index	SOG
Archdeaconry Court of Surrey	GLRO
Commissary Court of Surrey	GLRO
Indexed 1752-1858 by Cliff Webb	
Peculiar Court of the Archbishop of Canterbury in the Deanery of Croydon (included Newington)	Lambeth Palace Library

Wills after 1858 have all been proved at the Principal Registry of the Family Division where there is also an index.

A horse drawn hearse in Lynton Road, Bermondsey c.1900.

Addresses

Southwark Local Studies Library
211 Borough High Street
LONDON SE1 1JA
Tel 0171 403 3507

Newington Reference Library
155-157 Walworth Road
LONDON SE17 1RS
Tel 0171 708 0516

Southwark Registrar's Department
32 Peckham Road
LONDON SE5 8UB
Tel 0171 525 7556

Southwark Cemeteries Department
Camberwell New Cemetery
Brenchley Gardens
LONDON SE23
Tel 0171 639 3121

Greater London Record Office (GLRO)
40 Northampton Road
LONDON EC1R OHB
Tel 0171 332 3820

Public Record Office (PRO)*
Census and wills
Chancery Lane
LONDON WC2 1AH
Other records
Ruskin Avenue
KEW
Surrey TW9 4DU
Tel 0181 876 3444

General Register Office*
St Catherine's House,
Kingsway
LONDON WC2B 6JP
Copy certificates are available from
General Register Office
Smedly Hydro
Trafalgar Road
SOUTHPORT
Merseyside PR8 2HH

Principal Registry of the Family Division
Somerset House
Strand
LONDON WC2R 4LB

Guildhall Library
Aldermanbury
LONDON EC2P 2EJ
Tel 0171 606 3030

Lambeth Archives Department
Minet Library
52 Knatchbull Road
LONDON SE5 9QY
Tel 0171 926 6076

*The General Register Office and PRO Census Reading Room are to move to 1, Drummond Gate, LONDON SW1V 2QQ in 1997.

Surrey Record Office
County Hall
Penrhyn Road
Kingston-upon Thames
Surrey KT1 2DN
Tel 0181 541 9065

Society of Genealogists (SOG)
14 Charterhouse Buildings
LONDON EC1
Tel 0171 251 8799

The Church of Jesus Christ of Latter-day Saints
64 Exhibition Road
LONDON SW7
Tel 0171 589 8561

Lambeth Palace Library
LONDON SE1 7JU

Joining a family history society will put you in touch with other family historians locally. It will give you the chance to swap stories of successes and frustrations and provide ideas for further research. The society which includes this area, with a Southwark Group meeting at Southwark Local Studies Library is the
East Surrey Family History Society
Rosemary Turner
27 Burley Close
LONDON SW16 4QQ.

Also active locally is the West Surrey Family History Society
Mrs Sylvia McQuire
Deer Dell, Botany Hill Sands
FARNHAM
Surrey GU10 1LZ.

The umbrella group is the Federation of Family History Societies
Benson Room
Birmingham and Midland Institute
Margaret Street
BIRMINGHAM B3 3BS.